MW01505531

How to Recharge Your Nonprofit's Board of Directors

A Handbook for Restructuring and Re-Energizing Your Nonprofit's Board of Directors

By Jim Schell

Co-author of Small Business for Dummies

For distribution information please call

Lights On Publishing
541-788-7137
Bend, Oregon

Printed in the United States of America

Contents

About the Author

Jim Schell writes about what he has lived. Following graduation from the University of Colorado, subsequent 55 years of work/fun has resulted in four successful careers—the first as an entrepreneur, followed by writer, nonprofit creator-and-fixer, and finally, today, a hybrid of the first three which he calls his Giveback Career. Jim's entrepreneurial career, mostly in Minneapolis, included three for-profit startups and one for-profit turnaround. The third of the startups resulted in a 200-employee business. His writing career, still ongoing, has accounted for six published books, the sixth of which was the 1996 co-authorship of *Small Business for Dummies,* still one of the nation's leading books on small business. The nonprofit career which followed shortly after Jim's 1994 relocation to Bend, Oregon, includes three nonprofit turnarounds and six nonprofit startups. Fast forward to today, Jim is totally immersed in his Giveback Career which, he surmises, is just getting started and has a long way to go.

While traversing his various careers, Jim got a taste of the magic that happens when nonprofits merge with the entrepreneurial sector's best. He shares the secret to making that happen in the following pages. We'll learn firsthand how to infuse a nonprofit's board of directors, and hence the nonprofit, with an entrepreneurial culture, one dedicated to continued organizational growth. That dedication, according to Jim, results in the nonprofit serving a "larger audience with an expanded footprint through constantly-evolving services."

What would happen if all of a community's nonprofits blended their outstanding missions with a culture of entrepreneurship? One can only imagine …

Dedicated to those people whose primary job is making our community—and our nation—a better place to live. May you and your organization enjoy the success you deserve.

Preface
Why I Am Qualified to Write this Book

Several years ago, one of our local nonprofit's financial situation was bleak. Back-office procedures were in disarray. The executive director (ED) was burned out, and the prior board of directors had lost control of the organization.

I was asked to lead a turnaround and accepted the challenge. I'd spearheaded several nonprofit turnarounds before, and this particular one played a key role in the infrastructure of my adopted hometown of Bend, Oregon. Similar to every nonprofit (and for-profit) turnaround, the first three tasks that needed attention:

1. Resolve the cash flow situation.
2. Find a smokin' hot person to be the ED.
3. Begin assembling an all-star board of directors, people who would play a major, hands-on role in rebuilding the organization.

After resolving #1 (by raising $100,000 within the community) and #2 (by promoting one of the deserving staff members to executive director), I began the search for a board of directors. I had no goal in mind other than to assemble a random collection of extra-special people with identifiable skill sets. In the case of our organization, those skill sets would include experience in events, fundraising, marketing/branding, program management, finance and legal.

Several months into the board-building project, I read an intriguing magazine article stating the startling fact that the typical board of one successful national nonprofit organization had anywhere from 20 to 40 board members. *What could I effectively do with that many board members?* I wondered. Most boards I had been involved in have had seven to nine members. Even that can be too many if the board members are not synergistic or collaborative, a situation that is all-too-often the case. If I had my way (I'm a serial entrepreneur by trade and you know what, uh, control freaks people like me can be), my perfect board would be comprised of three close friends who, after accepting the fiduciary responsibility inherent in overseeing a nonprofit, would nod their heads once every three months at a quarterly meeting and stay out of my way.

Despite my dubious opinion of boards, I knew we needed one, and a good one at that. There was much work to be done, a lot of which was outside my skill set. I decided I'd build a younger, more involved board. For starters, millennials are the primary demographic served by the nonprofit I'd been hired to help. Also, I'm a certified old guy and much of what goes on in the millennial world is Greek to me. Finally, I knew I wanted a board made up of people with varied skills. Despite what I had read, I didn't need 20 of them, or so I thought at the time. Still, the notion persisted. What could be done with a board of 20 or more people, especially if those people were young, skilled and motivated to get things done?

From that inauspicious, accidental beginning, the idea for an Entrepreneurial Team Model was born. The evolution was an organic process. It took at least six months for the vision to fully develop, the players to be drafted and for the team members to get to know each other and properly bond. Once the pieces fell in place, however, the results were shocking. Shockingly awesome, that is.

I've served on a number of nonprofit boards over my career. I've even been an executive director with a board of my own. Yet I've never witnessed anything in the art of nonprofit board-building like what happens when hand-picked teams of people—initially conscripted because of their skill sets (as opposed to their financial wherewithal or their love of the mission)—are granted the latitude to determine and execute the decisions that will make or break the organization.

The result of that scenario is chronicled in this book.

Introduction

For those readers who head straight to the Introduction to determine what a book is about and whether or not it's worth reading, allow me to help you solve that problem right off the bat. This book is about building a board of directors, one that includes two elements that all volunteer-based nonprofits struggle to develop: *accountability* and *execution*. I've dubbed the model that evolved from my work in the field the Entrepreneurial Team Model, the essence of which involves forming small teams of board members within the overall board. Each team is then granted the responsibility and the authority to develop and execute its own innovative ideas without having to get consensus from the rest of the board. In short, the teams drive the board, not the other way around.

The coolest thing about this Entrepreneurial Team Model? It doesn't require board chairs to spend their valuable time pleading, cajoling or following-up in order to get things done. Such unpleasant management activities will no longer be a part of their responsibilities. Instead, the culture of accountability and execution that permeates these boards will be driven by the team members themselves. What's more, the board experience will also turn out to be fun as the achievements pile up!

Intrigued? You should be. Read on.

Why This Model Is Needed

I live in Bend, Oregon, a community of 85,000 people. Literally hundreds of nonprofits grace our city's boundaries, ranging from social service providers to sports associations to investment clubs. Most of our nonprofits are designed to make our community a better place to live, and most of those are classified as 501(c)3s. Which means, by law, that most of those nonprofits must have a board of directors. By extension, this means that we have hundreds of boards of directors toiling away in our fair city.

Given several bad experiences I've had in the past, I've always wondered just how functional the typical board of directors is. I decided to find out from the person who knows our nonprofit landscape better than anyone else—our United Way executive director.

Similar to most U.S. communities of comparable and larger size, we have a United Way. The executive director of our United Way is a 30-year veteran in his position who knows his way around town, especially within the nonprofit and for-profit sectors. United Ways, as we all know, serve as sort of a philanthropic middleman, collecting monies from the private sector and awarding the proceeds to deserving nonprofit organizations, usually those with a social service mission. As a result, most respectable United Way executive directors, which ours certainly is, know and understand the nonprofit landscape from top to bottom. After all, that's part of the job. They're charged with making sure that the nonprofit recipients of the money handed out are deserving of, and will be protective of, the funds entrusted to them.

I shared a latte with our United Way executive director several months ago. In the course of our conversation, he made a comment that came as no surprise to me. "Jim," he said, "I would estimate that out of our region's top 100 nonprofits, no more than a dozen have what I would rate an excellent board of directors." The rest, he concluded, "range from mediocre to dysfunctional, with the vast majority residing somewhere in between."

He paused and then added, "It's your typical bell curve, except that it's slanted precariously to the right."

The #1 Reason Why Boards of Directors Succeed or Fail

My 20 years of nonprofit experience in Bend tells me that my United Way friend is spot on. And oh, these underperforming boards are so ripe for improvement. After all, a nonprofit's board of directors is, by far, the most important element of any nonprofit organization. That's because boards can, and almost always do, make or break the organization. They make or break the organization because they have the final word regarding all that goes on, from hiring the executive director, to keeping her on track, to firing her, not to mention everything in between.

The success or failure of a board of directors is basically a function of two board members' attributes at work:

1. Their collective skills.
2. Their motivation.

If the organization's board members have the necessary skill sets and are motivated to work together, then suddenly the nonprofit has a team of talented people committed to achieving its mission. Which means, among other things, the executive director is no longer working alone.

I'll say it again; the board of directors is unquestionably *the* most important piece of the nonprofit puzzle, much more so than the executive director. After all, the board hires and fires the ED, not the other way around. Make no mistake about it. The universal law of any organization, which says that an organization will rise and fall as a result of the quality of its leadership, applies to nonprofits. No matter how good the ED is, she cannot overcome a mediocre or dysfunctional board. This applies to nonprofits and it applies to public corporations. It even applies to nations. After all, no entity, large or small, can outperform its leadership.

How about Your Nonprofit? Do You Have a Dysfunctional Board of Directors?

I use the term *dysfunctional* to describe what happens when a traditional board (or any board for that matter) with weak leadership and fractured membership exists. While the word dysfunctional should be self-describing, if your board includes more than one of the following characteristics, then you are, in my mind, situated in one stage or another of dysfunctionality:

1. Unpredictable attendance and frequent quorum shortfalls.
2. Board meetings lasting more than two hours.
3. The frequent need to have more than one board meeting per month.
4. Micromanagement of the ED by board members.
5. Heated arguments evolving between board members.
6. Board members frequently interrupting one another.
7. Cliques developing within the board.

8. Action items not being followed up on or, even worse, action items not being captured, making them impossible to follow up on.

9. Board members not being knowledgeable of the organization's financial condition.

10. Board meeting discussions dominated by one or two individuals.

11. Fractured voting that often results in split decisions.

12. Excessive turnover of board members not serving out their terms.

13. Board members not participating in fundraising events and activities.

The list could go on.

The Importance of a Top-Notch Board

Okay, so you've evaluated your board. Perhaps you've found it wanting but aren't sure that it's worth a shakeup. Looking at the impact, for better or worse, of an excellent nonprofit board may just change your mind.

Think about what happens when you have an excellent board and a mediocre ED The excellent board would assumedly be unhappy with the mediocre ED, whereupon it would replace her, assumedly with someone whose talents are on a par with the board's abilities.

What happens when you have a mediocre board and a mediocre ED? Why the board and the ED maintain the status quo, in which case the organization muddles on, mired in mediocrity.

Finally, what happens when you have an excellent ED and a mediocre board? The under-supported ED would be unhappy and restless, in which case she will ultimately go somewhere else where she can work with people of equal ability.

The lesson here? The success of a nonprofit starts and ends with the quality of its board.

Imagine what would happen in your community if the top 100 nonprofits suddenly upped their game measurably. Imagine the leverage to make a difference without having to fundraise one solitary dime. Imagine the collective good that would result.

Imagine!

Chapter 1
Three Keys to Making the Concept Work—
Execution, Accountability and Teams

"A key element of the Entrepreneurial Team Model's success is building a board that is made up of smaller intra-board teams instead of depending on individuals."

Let's begin this exploration into a new and better way to handle nonprofit boards of directors with my perception about how too many traditional nonprofit boards go about their business. Admittedly, my opinions are mostly informed by my own personal experiences coupled with what I hear from friends who also serve on boards along with my United Way executive director friend. I also know for a fact that there are several superstar boards in my community, all of which have a strong ED and most of which have strong board chairs who often serve for more than the usual two years. Still, most nonprofit boards squander the opportunity to have a meaningful impact on their communities. Here's why:

In my mind, a traditional board of directors is one in which the entire board makes all the important decisions. The resulting necessity for the entire board to participate in the meaty decisions means that most board meetings evolve into lengthy discussions of the pros and the cons regarding the topic *du jour*. So board meetings become long and protracted, and the energy level of the attendees sags as the meetings drag on without much getting accomplished. Sadly, these boards succeed or fail based on the degree of collaboration and commitment of the board chair and the executive director rather than the board as a whole. Too often the 80/20 rule is alive and well when board meetings are ineffective—80 percent of the board's work gets done by 20 percent of its members, usually the board chair working in tandem with the ED.

The process is further stymied by the fact that, all too often, the ED feels that she has nine (or however many) bosses as board members, many of whom show up only at the monthly board meetings. As a result, the responsibility for the execution of decisions made at the board level is often either murky or rests entirely on the shoulders of the ED instead of being shared with board members. That's compounded by the fact that many traditional board members seem to believe that their work is finished after the monthly board meeting and that contributing two hours a month is enough. It's hard to blame them when you factor in the pain and suffering involved in so many typically inefficient board meetings.

I believe that a significant part of the success of any nonprofit board is the fun factor. If board meetings and board work are fun, then most board members will step up to the plate and contribute. If they aren't fun, then they won't. I can honestly say I've attended very few traditional board meetings that I would categorize as fun. On the other hand, I've attended very few entrepreneurial team meetings that weren't.

With that definition in mind (and thanks to Steve Jobs who believed in the magic of the number three), here are the three primary reasons why most traditional nonprofit boards underperform:

1. Failure to understand that it's execution, not ideas, that drive an organization's success.
2. Failure to build a culture of accountability within the board.
3. Failure to focus on the collaborative power of teams.

Let's take a deeper dive into these three reasons.

Reason #1: It's Execution, Not Ideas. That Drives an Organization's Success

Let's start by repeating one of my all-time favorite quotes from some long-forgotten sage:

> *It matters not what you say, think or believe. What matters is what you do.*

Or here's another long-time favorite, along the same lines:

> *Anyone who can take a shower can have a good idea. What matters is what happens after you towel off.*

The message of both these adages is, simply put, that execution is king. Good ideas, great intentions and heartfelt beliefs are nice, but if they aren't executed, what difference do they make? It doesn't matter, for instance, that you believe that poverty is wrong, that you can wax poetic on the subject of how wrong it is, or that you know exactly what needs to be done in order to alleviate it. What matters is whether you actually step up and *do* something about alleviating poverty. Once you get actively involved in a project or program designed to significantly impact poverty, and once you begin executing those projects or programs, all of sudden things get done and poverty gets impacted. A good idea has never resolved anything; only through execution can a difference be made.

Too many nonprofit boards of directors underperform because they don't understand that execution rules. Certainly they care about the nonprofit's mission, and of course they have all kinds of great ideas about what to do to accomplish that mission, but for whatever reason they can't make the hard part—the execution—happen.

This bias to inaction is not human nature. Rather, it's a symptom of something inherently wrong in the board-building process. The board doesn't get the quality of members it needs because too many people join nonprofit boards for the wrong reason. They join because:

- They love the mission. (Okay, so loving the mission is a good start, but it's only a beginning.)
- They want the board position to be part of their resume.
- Their employer wants them to get involved in the community.

The board members described above do not join a board of directors because they are committed to becoming a member of a functional team that assumes responsibility for getting things done. Rather, all too often, they expect someone else to take care of the execution. (I'm not talking about the actual get-your-hands-dirty execution, but rather the planning that goes into the execution.) This disconnect of expectations is a recipe for mediocrity. It's the difference between having one person (the executive director) working to convert an idea into a reality and 19 people (the size of my latest board) working together to support the ED.

Reason #2: Boards Need to Create a Culture of Accountability—Without It, Good Work Doesn't Get Done

Accountability, we're told, is the act of accepting responsibility for the execution of whatever tasks have been assigned. Without someone accepting the accountability to get things done, there's no assurance that those tasks will be completed on time or at all.

Ask any successful leader or manager what the top three elements of his or her organization's culture are, and nine times out of ten, somewhere in the top three will be *accountability*. It's hard to imagine a successful organization that doesn't include accountability as a key driver of its culture. In those nonprofit organizations where a culture of accountability doesn't exist, board chairs are forced to spend too much of their time reactively following up instead of proactively getting things done.

In a for-profit organization, a culture of accountability can be fairly easily nurtured since execution is part and parcel of the expectation of receiving a pay check and since termination is an expected outcome when an employee underperforms. However, since board members are essentially unpaid volunteers, building a culture of accountability is especially dicey in nonprofits, given that the person assigning the task has no leverage with the person he's assigning it to. Since volunteer board members don't depend on the organization's pay check, and since it's uncomfortable having to terminate a volunteer board member who isn't performing, there is no easy way to make a board member accountable.

Because the executive director serves at the whims of the board, she is not in a position to hold board members accountable. That task falls in the lap of the board chair, who is himself a volunteer. Thus, we have the situation of one volunteer trying to hold a group of other volunteers accountable. At best, a difficult situation for both parties. No wonder few board chairs have the time, the energy and/or the willingness to do what it takes to build an accountable culture within a board of directors.

Reason #3: Boards Focus on Individuals Rather Than on Teams

An organization, by definition, is a collection of individuals working together toward a common mission. In the end, however, it will not be a group of individuals, outstanding as they may be, who will make or break that organization. Rather, the way those individuals work together as a team will cause the organization to succeed or fail. Follow the fortunes of any sports team, and it becomes readily apparent that it's not the team with the best individuals that wins; it's the team that learns how to get those individuals to play together as a team.

Here are five reasons why teams always trump individuals:

1. Teams create synergy—the value of the sum becomes greater than the value of the parts.
2. Teams create competition, both within and outside the organization.
3. Teams create innovation through the melding of ideas and best practices.
4. Teams create a sense of collaborative achievement as people work together to achieve shared goals.
5. For most people, working with a team is more fun than working alone.

As we shall soon see, a key element of the Entrepreneurial Team Model's success is building a board that's made up of smaller intra-board teams rather than depending on individuals. Imagine the leverage that evolves when five or six teams actively work together and hold one another accountable. In essence, this combination of teamwork and accountability is what makes the Entrepreneurial Team Model so different from the traditional board of directors.

Chapter 2
The Entrepreneurial Team Model—
Why It Evolved

"Thanks to the Entrepreneurial Team Model, the doers grow from one person (the ED) to 19 people."

As explained earlier, the Entrepreneurial Team Model was not a planned outcome when I started building the board that led to writing this book. Rather, the model organically evolved. I did, however, have four objectives in mind when I originally set out to build a board of director's model that encouraged collaboration and accountability. Those four objectives were to:

1. Increase the degree of commitment and participation of the board members.
2. More actively involve millennial and early Gen X members.
3. Develop an entrepreneurial, innovative and accountable culture within the board.
4. Better leverage the time, energy and talents of the ED.

A brief overview of those four objectives and how they contribute to the success of the Entrepreneurial Team Model follows.

1. Increase the Degree of Commitment and Participation of the Board Members

An integral part of the Entrepreneurial Team Model is the intra-board team meetings that take place outside of the monthly board meetings. There are no hard-and-fast requirements as to how often these intra-board teams should meet; each team determines its own meeting schedule, depending upon its workload. Typically, most of these intra-board teams will meet at least once a month between the full board meetings, with some meeting more often as needs dictate. From these meetings will come the direction of the organization within that team's discipline, which could be, for instance, fundraising, programs, events or marketing.

What is happening here is that by ceding decision-making responsibility to the smaller (typically four-person) teams, the responsibility—and thus the commitment—of the team members increases.

2. More Actively Involve Millennial and Younger Gen X Community Members

In traditional nonprofits, at least those I've been involved in, the majority of the organization's board members have been older Gen Xers, boomers and Silent Generation members, even when the people the nonprofit serves are millennials and Gen Xers. It makes little sense to me that boards are made up of only us older folks (I'm a Silent Generation guy), despite the fact—or so the thinking goes—that we elders can write the biggest checks and supposedly have more free time to spend on board activities.

I've learned that millennials make first-rate board members if given the opportunity to work without close supervision and if not required to write big checks (or with some, *any* checks). Besides having fresh ideas and a totally different outlook on the world, the millennials bring with them an understanding of today's technologies and social media tools. Thus, they are better able to communicate with people in their age group. They also, obviously, have a better understanding of millennials, who are oftentimes on the receiving end of the organization's mission.

My initial foray into the Entrepreneurial Team Model included a combination of all four generations (Silent, boomers, Gen X and millennials), with a heavy bias toward the millennials. That mix turned out to provide a melting pot of innovation and new ideas, not to mention a learning experience for us all as board members from the different generations worked together as a team.

3. Develop an Entrepreneurial, Innovative and Accountable Culture

As discussed earlier, the formation of entrepreneurial teams and the subsequent delegation of decision-making responsibilities to those teams play an important role in the success of this model. By delegating the decision-making responsibility to the teams (as opposed to the decision-making being made by the board as a whole) and by insuring that each team is made up of people with skills in their particular discipline, the result will be the development of:

- An entrepreneurial culture that is not afraid to try new ideas.
- A bias toward innovation resulting from the freedom that the teams have to create their own destiny.
- An accountable culture, thanks to the peer pressure that comes from the teams being responsible to the rest of the board for the strategy and decisions within their area of expertise.

4. Better Leverage of the Executive Director's Time, Energy and Talent

With the traditional board model, the nonprofit's organization chart often has, in effect, one executive director working for nine (or however many) board members. The board members offer suggestions to the ED on ways to enact her ideas, whereupon the ED bids the board farewell for a month and then reports back at the next regularly scheduled board meeting. In this model then, the ED is the sole doer and does not have an opportunity to leverage the get-things-done assets of her board.

This traditional scenario contrasts with the Entrepreneurial Team Model, in which the executive director becomes a working member of each of the internal teams. This means that the board has multiple teams of anywhere from two to four members doing the planning and related heavy lifting on whatever project they are pursuing. Thanks to the accountable culture that develops as part of the Entrepreneurial Team Model, the board members now become more actively involved. The result is that instead of having one ED doing the planning and then leading the execution, all the board members are now involved. Suddenly, the doers in an Entrepreneurial Team organization grow from one person (the ED) to 19 people

Now that we have discussed the philosophy behind creating a board using the Entrepreneurial Team Model, it's time to discuss another key element of the concept—what makes them work.

Chapter 3
Introducing the Entrepreneurial Team Model

"In the Entrepreneurial Team Model, the responsibility for decision-making is being shifted from the board as a whole down to its entrepreneurial teams."

The Entrepreneurial Team Model is essentially an intra-board team approach to running a board of directors with an entrepreneurial bent. Each board member is assigned to an intra-board team; each of those teams includes board members with skill sets that align with the other members of their team. These intra-board teams are then given the responsibility of providing strategic direction, tactical assistance, and applicable decision-making within their team's area of expertise. In essence, the responsibility for decision-making is being shifted from the board as a whole down to its entrepreneurial teams.

Of course, by virtue of the fiduciary responsibility that every member of a nonprofit board of directors agrees to when joining the board, there must be a caveat to this delegation of decision-making. The caveat is that the finance team (which usually includes two members, one of which is the board chair) has the sole right to veto any decisions that evolve from any of the intra-board teams. The finance team may only exercise its veto right when it determines that a team's decision could be detrimental to the long-term financial sustainability of the organization. Other than the finance team's veto responsibility, all board decisions emanate from the teams themselves.

Each of the intra-board teams charged with such responsibilities as events, program development, fundraising, marketing and membership is made up of four (sometimes more, sometimes less) members. In addition to those four-member teams, there is also the finance team we discussed, a one-member legal team, and finally, the board chair position. Later, in Chapter 6, we'll see exactly what a typical 19-member board looks like.

The result of this transfer of accountability, from the overall board to the intra-board teams, is a deepened commitment by the board members. With the increased decision-making responsibilities of the teams, individual board members now have more skin in the game.

Why the Entrepreneurial Team Model Works

Due to the collaborative nature of the Entrepreneurial Team Model, there are a number of reasons why this approach will consistently out-produce the traditional board model. Those reasons include:

- The increased output that results when teams of people with like-minded skills work together toward a common solution.
- The granting of decision-making responsibility to teams of capable people with synergistic skill sets.
- The bonding that results from board members being part of a functioning, responsible and successful team.

- Sheer numbers; since most boards range from 7 to 15 members, a 19-member board simply has more horsepower.

The really, truly secret sauce of the Entrepreneurial Team Model, however, can be boiled down to a single reason: the tangible element of good, old-fashioned peer pressure that develops when teams of talented and motivated people respectfully compete—yes, compete—with other teams of talented, motivated people.

Here's an example of how this intra-board competition works. Let's say the chair of the events team stands up in front of his peers at the monthly board meeting and outlines an exciting new idea that his team has developed during the course of the month. Would then, the next team chair on the agenda, let's say the chair of the fundraising team, stand up and have little or nothing to report? Not a chance given the kind of competitive, successful people that make up a properly-assembled entrepreneurial team. In this example, the fundraising team chair knows from past experience that the events team (along with the other teams) will have their usual array of cool ideas and successful outcomes to report at each board meeting. Such peer pressure motivates her to, at the very least, keep up with the other teams, if not outperform them.

Thus. peer pressure becomes the primary driver of each team's efforts, especially in the early stages of the entrepreneurial board's development. In the above example, the fundraising team knows that it's going to be measured by the rest of the board against the events team (and ultimately against all of the teams).

The accountability that results from this element of peer pressure will become an integral part of the culture of the board. Each team will inherently be holding itself accountable to make sure that its output measures up to what the other teams are doing.

Imagine, if you will, a board model where accountability and results are built into the system. Imagine a system where execution is not dependent upon the board chair having to follow up, or upon some other form of policing, since accountability is now a part of the model itself.

Sound like a dream? Well maybe, but it's a dream that can become a reality. Eventually, given the string of successes that will stem from utilizing this collaborative-based team model, the adrenalin that results from a group of committed people knocking the ball out of the park can provide unstoppable motivation. Success will become its own reward.

And, if all this imagining isn't enough, there is one other positive result that originates with an accountable board that's making things happen. The accountable culture that develops will, by osmosis, trickle down to the staff. This is because culture always starts at the top—the board sets the cultural tone and the staff will follow, a situation which will happen for better or for worse.

Chapter 4
Benefits of the Entrepreneurial Team Model

"The Entrepreneurial Team Model offers many benefits, the foremost of which is that it forces all the board members to get involved."

In addition to the results that will evolve from the sheer numbers of 19 (or more) talented members working together as a team, there are additional tangible benefits of the Entrepreneurial Team Model. Those benefits include:

Fostering Entrepreneurial Solutions to Problems and Opportunities

The adjective *entrepreneurial* implies such cultural traits as:

- Thinking outside of the box, aka innovating.
- A willingness to take risks amid a culture that allows failure.
- A bias to action, i.e., a propensity to make things happen and get projects done sooner rather than later.

Inviting Increased Participation by Board Members

Members of the entrepreneurial teams, by virtue of their intermittent meetings, will expend more time and effort on the affairs of the organization because:

- They feel more empowered.
- The system, by its very nature, makes them more motivated to perform.
- The frequency of the team meetings, along with the board meetings, simply requires more time.

Expanding the Role of Board Members

Instead of the role that traditional board members typically play, i.e., advising and planning, the Entrepreneurial Team Model adds *doing* to the board's mix.

Attracting Millennials and Young Professionals

Millennials and young professionals are, by their very nature, meeting-adverse, particularly when talk is king and things don't get done. They especially dislike ineffective meetings because they are busy building their careers and raising young families. For them to continue taking time away from those two pursuits they must see tangible outcomes. This issue is one of the primary reasons why millennials and young professionals don't consider joining such traditional community organizations as Rotaries and Chambers of Commerce.

Additionally, for better or for worse, millennials prefer to do things their way. The Entrepreneurial Team Model is built to foster such independence.

Utilizing the Advantage of Sheer Numbers

When event time comes around, as it does at least once a year for most nonprofits, the advantage of having 19 board members inviting and/or bringing guests, rather than, say, nine members, is obvious.

Leveraging the Time and Energy of the Executive Director

Instead of being only an implementer, the ED now becomes a coordinator *and* an implementer, and can spend her time coordinating (and thereby leveraging) the talents of both her staff and the board members.

Chapter 5
The Three People Who Make the Entrepreneurial Team Model Work

"People make up boards and people build them, without the right people leading the board-building process, the board will under-perform. Or worse."

No matter what board of director model you favor, boards don't build themselves. People build them. In the case of the Entrepreneurial Team Model, it takes the combined talents of three key people to build a board. So, again with appreciation to Steve Jobs, here's yet another three-bullet-point outline.

The Three Keys to a Successful Entrepreneurial Team Board:

1. An insightful convener(s)—a person(s) with a broad community network who can attract talented board members. The term *convener* comes from the Latin word *convenire* meaning to unite, be suitable, agree, and/or assemble.

2. A board chair that supports the Entrepreneurial Team Model, is an excellent facilitator of meetings, and knows when to get out of the way.

3. A competent and committed ED who is able to work and communicate with the board chair and with the teams.

Let's look closely at these three key roles.

The Convener

Every successful entrepreneurial team must have a person or persons behind it with a broad, far-reaching network from which he/she can attract and conscript board members who have the skill sets the nonprofit needs to be successful. In addition to accessing that network, the convener's role must not only be to identify those potential board members, but also to convince them to join the board. To do that, the convener must be credible and convincing, in the process developing excitement about the nonprofit's mission and the opportunity to work on a hand-picked, all-star team.

A successful convener understands that most communities include two demographics of potential board members:

1. Older, experienced community members who are usually members of the boomer or Silent Generation.
2. The younger set; i.e., the millennials and Gen Xers.

The convener(s) must have a network that includes both demographics, and must have the credibility to be able to approach and engage prospective board members from those two groups. If the convener doesn't have connections in both networks, he must recruit a sub-convener who does.

Yes, the convener could be the executive director if that person is aggressive and well-connected enough, but more likely the convener will be the person who either already is—or ultimately will turn out to be—the board chair. If the board chair doesn't have the network within the two age groups, his first task should be to recruit a board member who does have a network in both demographics.

The Board Chair

The board chair's primary role in the Entrepreneurial Team Model is not to make key decisions—the teams will do that. And it is not to hold board members accountable—the teams will do that, too. Rather, one of his handful of primary roles is to effectively facilitate the board meetings. In order to properly facilitate a team of skilled, successful board members, the board chair must possess a high degree of team-building skills. After all, the board's entrepreneurial teams presumably include members from varied demographics who are oftentimes, at the outset, strangers to one another. Strong facilitators usually have a background of running meetings, normally in the private sector. Facilitation is more science than art, and many aspects of it don't come naturally to most of us. But it's a skill that every board chair can—and should—study and work on.

Unlike the board chair in a traditional nonprofit board setting, the Entrepreneurial Team's board chair's duty is NOT to make, or pass judgement on, board decisions unless he and the finance team chair believe that the financial sustainability of the organization could be challenged by a team's decision. Instead, the board chair's duties now include, in addition to facilitation, such activities as cheerleading, problem solving, and managing the executive director.

Of course, one key element that remains constant in the role of any board, be it entrepreneurial or traditional, is the board's assumption of fiduciary responsibility. While the assumption of fiduciary responsibility is ultimately the duty of the board as a whole, in the Entrepreneurial Team Model the oversight of it rests with the board chair and the finance team chair. Certainly, the board as a whole assumes the final responsibility, but much as with a traditional board of directors, the day-to-day oversight comes from the finance team.

The #1 skill required of any board chair in the Entrepreneurial Team Model is the ability to facilitate a group of people, in this case a high-octane board of talented people consisting of varying demographics. It's also desirable, although not necessary, that the board chair be an entrepreneur, either current or past. (Who better to understand the entrepreneurial mindset than an already-vetted entrepreneur?) Finally, the board chair also needs to be at ease with change, as there will likely be pushback from the community as a result of the change inherent in transitioning from a traditional board to an entrepreneurial team board.

The Executive Director

While the executive director certainly plays an important role in the organization, it's difficult if not impossible for an ED to overcome a weak board. Thus, the building of a quality board must come first. Once the board is in place, filling the ED position follows.

Successful execution of the entrepreneurial team concept requires a fresh outlook from the executive director. Not unlike the role of a coach or a CEO, the ED must view her position as it relates to the board as a managerial opportunity designed to leverage the skills of the 19 talented board members.

The result of this change in perception is that the ED will spend much more time working with the board in the Entrepreneurial Team Model than she would in the traditional nonprofit. In addition to her normal duties of managing her staff and resolving day-to-day problems, she also has the unique goal of maximizing the output of her team of 19 talented volunteers. She may work for the board, but managed properly, the board can also be her most productive asset.

With that in mind, the #1 responsibility of the executive director in the Entrepreneurial Team Model is to manage that asset by coordinating the activities and outcomes of the teams. If an entrepreneurial team board has, say, 19 members, the leverage of those members represents a huge potential to the nonprofit. While it's the board chair that facilitates the monthly (or bi-monthly or quarterly) meetings of that asset, the role of managing the coordination between the teams falls to the executive director. The ED must be able to weave together the activities of the various teams, similar to what she must do with her staff members.

The executive director should attend all of the team meetings and work closely with each team as they create and execute their ideas and plans. Since the ED is the only person outside of the team members who attends the meetings, her role must be to coordinate the outcomes of the teams and make sure that silos don't develop between the teams. Silos arise when groups of people forget that they're part of a team and go about doing their work independently.

Typically, since the executive director is actively involved in the team meetings, any action items that result from those meetings will not be enacted without the assistance of the ED. This helps in assuring that team decisions are not going to be made that the ED doesn't agree with. Also, since the ED is, in fact, involved in the decision-making process, she is most likely to have the buy-in needed to forge successful outcomes from the team meetings.

So now the key players are in place and the stage is set to start assembling the board. In the following chapter, we'll see how that's done.

Chapter 6
Getting Started – Assembling the Board

"It's an immutable fact—everything must start somewhere and everything must start with someone. Assembling an entrepreneurial board is no exception. That somewhere is within the infrastructure of your own nonprofit and that someone is your organization's convener."

Before setting out to assemble your board, it's essential that your board's convener, whoever that person is, understand the concept that a nonprofit essentially operates like a for-profit business. The only major difference between the two is the way in which they're taxed. The nonprofit has all the same nuances at work as does the for-profit. Both entities have cash flow, and expenses, and revenues, and capital expenditures, and employees. They also both have a revenue-generation function. In the for-profit world that function is called sales; in the nonprofit world, it's known as fundraising or development. From a bookkeeping standpoint, the chart of accounts for a nonprofit and a for-profit are similar—only the account names have been changed.

The adage *no money, no mission* illustrates the importance of understanding the concept behind the way a nonprofit business must operate. In essence, with any nonprofit the money must come first;

only then can the mission follow. To those of us who have spent a majority of our career in the for-profit world, this is no surprise. Like it or not, the availability of money—aka cash—is the heartbeat of any organization from which everything else flows. After all, cash or any other asset that can be converted into cash within 30 days (in essence the organization's liquidity) is always the first place to look when evaluating the health of an organization, be it for-profit or nonprofit.

Remembering and reinforcing that concept when forming your board will help ensure the financial health of your nonprofit organization and its mission.

Building Your Board – Take Your Time

Allow six months or more to build your board. Don't rush the process. It's better to have one or more of the teams shorthanded for a period of time than to fill it with a team member who doesn't fit. After all, it's downright painful, not to mention bad public relations, to have to terminate a non-performing board member. On the other hand, it's even worse to retain a non-contributing board member and have him drag the board and his team down. Don't worry if one or more of your teams are slow to fill up. As those teams and your board grow, the teams will often find and recruit their missing members from within their own networks.

Who Should the Board Members Be?

What this no-money, no-mission adage means to the person (or persons) doing the convening of the board is that the #1 criterion when looking for board members should be that the majority of the board has an organizational background. While it certainly makes sense to have several board members who are mission zealots, at least 80 percent of the board should be comprised of people who understand how a business and/or a nonprofit, small or large, operates. Once such board members are in place, the mission of the nonprofit can be assimilated.

It's important to remember that it's not necessary to build an entrepreneurial team board with members who have a thorough knowledge and understanding of the organization's mission. Nor is it necessary to require that board members make sizable donations to the nonprofit as a prerequisite to becoming a board member, which is usually an integral part of the traditional pay-to-play board. Rather, the primary criteria for an entrepreneurial team board member should be the ability to think like a business person, which includes intuitively grasping a bottom-line mentality. A key component of a bottom-line mentality is comprehending, and thus assuming, the fiduciary responsibility that goes along with board membership. So it follows that the convener should be a business and/or nonprofit veteran with a broad network.

With such criteria in mind, here are the four steps involved in starting a board from scratch (more later on what to do if you're starting with an already-existing board):

1. Find the right convener or conveners.
2. Identify the teams your nonprofit needs and quantify the skill sets required to fill each of those teams.
3. Identify the networks required to find and recruit your new board members.
4. Sell the board and its mission to those prospective board members.

Outlining a Process for Building the Board

Let's take a deeper look at the execution of each of these four steps:

Step 1 – Find the right convener or conveners: Someone has to start the process of building (or re-building) the board, be it an initial convener who will do all of the hands-on convening himself, a team of two or more conveners, or someone who will lead the search to locate that initial convener(s). This someone would, most likely, be the board chair, although he/she could also be a major donor, a board member or even the executive director herself.

If the convener is not the board chair and is starting the board from scratch, the board chair position should be the first to be filled. Once the board chair is identified, he should also become one of the conveners. For purposes of following these four steps, it's assumed that at least one of the initial conveners is the board chair.

The convener should begin the board-building process by searching his network for a person or two—we'll call them sub-conveners—with ties to network sectors that the primary convener doesn't have. For instance, the convener (who as stated previously should be a business owner, general manager, CEO, or nonprofit veteran) should tap his network for sub-conveners who have networks within, say, the marketing sector or the event-planning sector, or with people who have fundraising skills. From that point, each sub-convener could then be named a team chair and build her own marketing team, event team, or fundraising team. In a perfect scenario, once each team chair is identified, those persons would be responsible for building his/her own team. (More on identifying the board's teams in Step 2.)

If the intent is to include millennials and early Gen Xers on the board (highly recommended), and the convener's network is in the traditional business or nonprofit sector, finding a sub-convener with a network in the new economy business sector is imperative. (Traditional sector businesses are those businesses which sell products and/or services that are consumed locally, while new economy sector businesses are those that sell their products and/or services outside of the community or region. Traditional businesses are typically the older, mature, established businesses of the community, e.g., Rotary and Chamber members for instance, while new economy businesses are the younger, newer businesses. Examples of traditional sector businesses include car dealers, real estate developers and retail shop owners, while examples of new economy sector businesses include tech, internet and science-related companies).

The ideal board then would have a vibrant and eclectic mixture of young and old (with a bias toward young), male and female, new economy and traditional economy, and would obviously include a variety of skills in order to fill its teams. Eclectic is good in the board-building world, not only because it's advantageous to have all the demographic bases covered, but because the success of a team feeds off its diversity. A team of eclectic people is more creative and innovative than a team of people who are all from the same demographic.

Step 2 – Identify the teams and quantify the skill sets needed to be part of those teams: The teams needed to fill out your board will depend on the mission and business model of your nonprofit. For instance, a membership-based nonprofit would require a membership team, while a food-kitchen nonprofit would not. Here is a general list of teams that might be part of an entrepreneurial board's infrastructure (a larger organization might need all the following teams while smaller organizations might require only four or five):

- **Finance Team:** Every sophisticated board needs at least one CPA as a member. The CPA and the board chair would then constitute the finance team. As mentioned earlier, this team, among other key duties, has veto powers over the decisions made by all the other teams. In addition to that key power, the finance team also reviews the organization's financials and makes appropriate recommendations as relates to the board's fiduciary responsibility.

- **Legal Team:** Every nonprofit board also needs an attorney as a member. A single attorney can constitute the legal team and will make recommendations on board issues that might have legal implications, as well as assume responsibility for keeping the bylaws up to date.

- **Fundraising & Revenue Generation Team:** The fundraising & revenue generation team consists of people who have contacts with the community's current and potential donors, and who also have connections within the business sector. This team should ideally be made up of people with experience in fundraising, people who are comfortable asking for money (something many board members don't like doing). In addition to soliciting donations, the fundraising team will also be responsible for developing donor databases and creating stewardship strategies. This team should include a mixture of members from the various demographics, i.e., millennial, Gen X, baby boomer and Silent Generation, to assure that all the demographic networks are covered.

In addition to the typical fundraising needs that are endemic to most nonprofits, some nonprofits don't just rely on charitable fundraising to generate revenue. These other fundraising techniques include such revenue generators as auctions, thrift stores, golf tournaments and grant writing. Finding team members with experience in any of these disciplines would be a bonus.

- **Marketing Team:** Marketing team members would include individuals who are either employees of ad agencies and/or marketing firms, marketing freelancers, or marketing directors from within a business. This team is responsible for such functions as branding, messaging, social media, public relations and website development. In addition to creating the various content described above, the marketing team, by virtue of the fact that what it does may impact other teams, must also be able to work closely with members of all the board's teams and the staff.

- **Program Team:** The program team develops and assures proper execution of the various programs that deliver the organization's mission. Oftentimes, program team members come from organizations and/or businesses that typically partner with the nonprofit. Program team members can range from owners and employees of businesses that typically employees of school districts, park and rec departments, and other service organizations that deal with your nonprofit on a regular basis.

- **Events Team:** The events team develops the annual event calendar and works with the nonprofit's staff in creating and strategizing individual events. Every community has a network of event freelancers and people in the event-staging business. This network should be tapped when building the events team.

- **Membership Team:** For those nonprofits that are membership-based, the membership team develops plans and strategies designed to attract and retain members. Membership team members should have previous experience in membership organizations, either as a member themselves or from working on membership drives and/or committees.

Step 3 – Identify the networks required to find and sign new board members: Once the convener(s) and sub-convener(s) are selected and the appropriate teams have been identified, it's time to determine where to search for the board members who have the skills required to fill the teams. Similar to hiring new employees, the best board members are generally people who come from known networks.

In the early stages of building the board, those networks would obviously be those of the convener(s). As the board grows and the teams fill out, new team members will typically come from the networks of the sub-conveners and from those of the previously-conscripted board members. Typical networks to be tapped, in addition to the friends and business acquaintances of the convener(s), might include such organizations as the Rotary, the Chamber of Commerce, economic development nonprofits, other business/service groups, etc. These traditional organizations, however, will usually not yield younger, new economy board members. Rather these people tend to come from such harder-to-find organizations as technology associations, makers teams and a variety of smaller, industry-specific groups.

Even though finding these younger recruits is more challenging, in the interest of making a board as eclectic as possible, it's imperative that your community's new economy business sector be well represented. Early on in the board-building process, the strategy should be to locate a board member or two with new economy networks and then build from those networks. A 19-person board should have at least six new economy members, most if not all of whom will probably be millennials or early Gen Xers.

Step 4 – Sell the board and its mission to prospective board members: Once a potential board member has been identified, the final piece of the puzzle is to convince him/her to join your board and to want to become a member of one of its entrepreneurial teams. Obviously, selling the social mission of the nonprofit is important, but for many business people, even more important is being a part of an interesting, eclectic and talented group. Oftentimes the primary draw to becoming a board member is meeting and working alongside new people from different demographics and unrelated sectors.

Building a board can be a time-consuming process, oftentimes taking six months or more. As board members are conscripted and the teams are assembled, it's important that the board chair focus on keeping the board motivated and excited as the build-up progresses. Motivated and excited board members will be enthusiastic about spreading the word to prospective board members within their own networks, adding an even broader referral base to the process.

The board chair should appoint the team chairs as the board is growing, making sure to tap the most talented and competitive new board members for the respective chair positions. In subsequent years, team chairs will be identified and appointed by the team itself. However, it's essential in the board's early development that the newly-appointed chairs be armed with the skills and attitudes necessary to build a culture of friendly competitiveness within the board.

Chapter 7
Restructuring an Already Existing Board

"Transitions and restructures, by definition, lead to something new, and if you've read this far, you're assumedly seeking something new."

While having the convener(s) assemble a board from scratch is the ideal situation, as a practical matter most nonprofits, unless they're startups, won't be afforded that luxury. Rather, the convener(s) may have to restructure an existing board, plugging existing members into the newly-appointed teams. Even so, the process will be basically the same as if starting anew. Someone still has to serve as the convener (probably the board chair), the appropriate teams will need to be identified and those teams will have to be populated with skilled board members.

The biggest difference between starting a board from scratch and restructuring an existing board is that when restructuring a board, the convener(s) will first have to identify which of the current board members will fit into the Entrepreneurial Team Model and which teams those people should be assigned to.

In all likelihood when restructuring a board, some existing board members won't fit into any of the teams. Oftentimes, those board members will self-identify as not being a fit and will choose to leave the board on their own. But occasionally, the board chair will have to make the difficult decision about whether to place an existing board member on a team anyway (thereby weakening the team) or ask that person to leave the board.

Organizational and Situational Evolution

Whether starting a board or restructuring one, this probably won't be the only time your board is going to change. Organizations shift with the passing of time. When organizations change, the infrastructure of the board must change too.

In one Entrepreneurial Team board I worked with, following a year of what was essentially a turnaround, we determined that the fundraising team and the marketing team needed to be combined. The reasoning behind this decision was that key functions of the marketing team, in the early stage of the turnaround, had included such tasks as branding, messaging and positioning. Once those restructuring tasks had been addressed and resolved, the need for the marketing team's services were primarily directed to promoting the fundraising team's programs and events.

The role of the board chair will also change as the organization's situational needs evolve. In the turnaround example cited above, in the early stages, as the organization worked its way through a severe cash flow problem, the chair's role was primarily that of a fundraiser. Once the cash flow issue was resolved, the chair's primary duty shifted to that of restructuring the board. Given the team-building requirements inherent in the restructuring and assembling of a new board, the chair's responsibilities changed to acting more as a cheerleader than a doer, as the teams assumed the doing functions themselves.

Hang On

Keep in mind that the transition and/or restructure involved in changing the culture of an organization are often tumultuous, which means the process of changing a board from a traditional model to an Entrepreneurial Team Model is likely to be fraught with conflict. But don't let that discourage you. Transitions and restructures, by definition, lead to something new, and if you've read this far, you're assumedly seeking something new.

So keep on reading, you're on the road to getting what you asked for.

Chapter 8
The Result - A Hypothetical
Entrepreneurial Team Board

"Each of the teams is charged with developing innovative and entrepreneurial solutions to the problems and opportunities that fall within their area of expertise."

While making substantive changes to your board won't be easy, seeing an entrepreneurial team board in action, even a hypothetical one, will help. As you read this chapter, however, please remember that no two boards are going to look the same, just as no two organizations, be they nonprofit or for-profit, will look the same. One size does not fit all where board building is concerned.

The following hypothetical board is just one of many examples of what an entrepreneurial team board can look like. This particular hypothetical board includes 19 board members only because the organization's mission called for four teams and the convener decided he needed four members on each team.

This hypothetical 19-member board includes six entrepreneurial teams and the board chair:

1. Program Team = 4 members + ED
2. Fundraising Team = 4 members + ED
3. Marketing Team = 4 members + ED
4. Events Team = 4 members + ED
5. Finance Team = 1 member + board chair + ED
6. Legal Team = 1 member
7. Board Chair = 1 member

Total = 19 members

Each of the above teams is charged with developing innovative and entrepreneurial solutions to the problems and opportunities that fall within their area of expertise. Teams are encouraged to try new approaches and stray out of their comfort zone in order to develop new and exciting directions for the organization. While failure most certainly is not encouraged, it's recognized as an integral part of creating an entrepreneurial culture and should be occasionally expected.

In addition to the above teams on this hypothetical board, other teams could include a volunteer team, a membership team or a board development team. Ad hoc teams are also encouraged where one-time events or capital fundraising drives might dictate a need.

The number of teams and the number of board members on each team will be driven solely by the needs of the organization. More teams, and thus more members, might be required for larger and more complex nonprofits. In addition, any or all of the individual teams might decide to include more than four members when a potential new contributing member appears after the team has been formed. There is nothing sacred about the four-members-per-team number. When new talent becomes available there's no reason not to increase the team members to five or more. It's important to remember that additional team members don't always have to be board members; they could simply be interested in volunteering for the team but not for the board.

Tips on Building an Effective Board

Here is a collection of hard-earned tips designed to help build a world-class board, a board that will raise the Entrepreneurial Team Model to yet another level:

- Each entrepreneurial team should have a chair or co-chairs to be appointed by the board chair or convener in the early stages of the board building process, and then elected by their team later on.

- The teams will meet on-demand, i.e., when the team chair (or co-chairs) determines that the team has issues it needs to discuss or act upon. Some months there might be multiple team meetings; other months there may be no meetings.

- It's important to remember that the teams do not recommend decisions and strategies. They actually make the decisions and determine the strategies—only the veto power of the finance committee can alter or trump those decisions. Thus, in effect, the board's teams drive the decision-making of the board rather than the board itself.

- Each team chair will report to the board at the regularly scheduled board meetings. These team reports will include such topics as new ideas the team is considering, new directions the team may be taking, and any formal decisions that have been made. These reports will not be for the purpose of asking for the board's approval, as board approval is implicit in the process, but rather will be to keep the board informed of the team's decisions.

- As discussed earlier, the executive director must be required to attend all team meetings. Her presence will ensure the efficient working of the Entrepreneurial Team Model as well as the ongoing collaboration and communication between the teams. In addition, it's imperative to the success of the concept that the ED be aware of, and thus fully supportive of, the decisions the teams make. Her support can, and will, only happen if she attends every meeting.

Board Donations

Many foundations require, as part of their grant protocol, that all of a nonprofit's board members make an annual donation, an issue that every board must address when recruiting new members. Since a typical entrepreneurial board's members may be younger than those of a traditional board, and since (as we've mentioned earlier) younger people typically don't have the financial resources that older ones do, it's recommended that an annual donation be allowed with no minimum.

It's further recommended that the executive director oversee the board donation process and that she be the only person in the organization who knows the size of each member's donation. In reality, even the board chair need not know which board member donated how much. After all, the size of a board member's donation pales in comparison to the good work he/she can eventually do as a part of a working team. It would be a shame to lose a potential superstar board member simply because she couldn't make what others might consider to be a significant donation.

Board Terms

The board chair should be allowed to serve at least two one-year terms consecutively, if, of course, the board chooses to re-elect him. After all, it takes time to adapt to the board chair position, especially given the uncharted waters of the newly-adopted Entrepreneurial Team Model. It seems a shame to limit a capable chair's service to only 12 months, at least half of which will be consumed by learning the vagaries of the job.

Meanwhile, all board members should be allowed to serve two three-year terms if they so choose. Since the Entrepreneurial Team Model requires its members to attend both board meetings AND team meetings, the time required to be a board member oftentimes means that only the very committed will agree to serve a second term.

Chapter 9
Making the Board Meetings Work

While the team meetings are where the important decisions are made, the monthly board meetings are the glue that binds the board to its mission.

It's one thing to build a great board; it's another to make it run smoothly and efficiently. While the team meetings are where the important decisions are made, the monthly board meetings are the glue that binds the board to its mission. Short, well-organized, snappy board agendas make the meetings fun as well as informative.

The agenda for a typical board meeting should look something similar to this:

1. Approval of minutes - All
2. Introductions (if any) - Board
3. Issues requiring board discussion and decision-making - Board chair
4. Staff and operational news from the past month - ED
5. Strategic and other news from the past month - Board chair
6. Team reports - Team chairs

7. Mission moment (a story of success.) - ED
8. Closing & review of board goals - Board chair

Board meetings should not last longer than 75 minutes. Budgeting the time to be spent on each agenda item will help keep the meeting on track. Since board consensus about decisions being made is no longer necessary, the discussions around those decisions should take a minimum amount of time, allowing the board to take care of its business in the allotted time. The first five agenda items as listed above, i.e., those that directly involve the board chair and the executive director, should not take more than 30 minutes of the meeting. These five agenda items are meant to be both informational and cheerleading in nature and are typically not conducive to long discussions. The bulk of the time will be spent on the team reports— the most important part of the meeting.

Team Meetings: Where the Work Gets Done

The board's real business is accomplished within the team meetings, thus the team reports part of the meeting should take the better part of the hour. It should be remembered that while board members can certainly make suggestions to the team chairs making the presentations, those comments should be largely inquisitive in nature (perhaps suggesting tweaks or changes to the team's direction), but not critical since the decision has, in effect, already been made.

Frequency of Board Meetings

Early on, following the initial assembling, the board should meet monthly in order to promote teambuilding, i.e., bringing the eclectic board members together to bond as a team. Since an entrepreneurial team's board meetings are primarily designed to be reporting in nature (as opposed to decision-making), once the board has bonded and the organization has matured, less-frequently scheduled board meetings are acceptable. Particularly in view of the added time commitment involved in the team meetings, the board may choose to meet once every other month, or once every quarter, instead of every month.

Since the entrepreneurial team board member will spend more time in meetings than the traditional board member, it's imperative to be considerate of her time. If the board has a number of millennial and early Gen X members, it should consider meeting over lunchtime as opposed to late in the afternoon or after dinner. Since a board consisting of younger board members often translates to board members with families and young children, protecting that post-5:00 p.m. family-time should be a priority.

This kind of sensitivity, initially generated by the board chair, will help cement the board as a whole.

Chapter 10
The Role and Responsibilities of the Board Chair

"One of the board chair's primary goals should be to develop a culture of friendly competition between the various teams."

It should be remembered that the 30,000-foot role of the board chair is to create and maintain an environment for the board to develop a creative, innovative and entrepreneurial culture. Thus, the chair is essentially building a culture within which the board can operate, as opposed to participating in the actual work that nonprofit boards are expected to do. Rather, that actual work should be the responsibility of the teams. The three primary tools the chair uses to create that supportive culture include cheerleading, planning (of agendas and strategy) and management (of the ED).

In reality, the responsibilities of an entrepreneurial team board chair are similar to those of the chair of a traditional board of directors. The difference is that the entrepreneurial team board chair 1) isn't required to work on, and drive, the organization's new programs and 2) isn't distracted by having to spend his time following up with board members. The program work gets done by the individual teams while the imbedded culture of accountability negates the need for following up.

Thus, the typical board chair's responsibilities are now to:

- Manage and mentor the ED, including preparation of the annual performance review.
- Plan and facilitate board meetings.
- Plan, organize and drive the organization's annual strategic planning efforts.
- Act as chief cheerleader for the board and its teams.
- In partnership with the ED, act as chief ambassador of the organization to the community at large.
- As is expected of all board members, approve the budget and assure that all legal and fiduciary responsibilities are met.
- Working with the ED, assure that all stakeholders are apprised of the organization's affairs.
- Assure that there is at least one capable candidate on the board who is able and willing to succeed him.
- Lead the board in recruiting capable board members.
- Where necessary, assess the performance of board members who are not contributing.
- Working with the finance team chair, assume the veto role when events, programs or ideas are generated that could have significant negative financial impact on the organization.
- Get out of the way of the teams, allowing them to be entrepreneurial and innovative.

Certainly there may be times when the board chair has an idea for an event, or a program, or a concept that he believes would benefit the organization. In such cases, he should present that idea to the applicable team chair who would then have the option to invite the board chair to be a guest at a team meeting and discuss the issue. At that time, the board chair would present his idea, while remaining respectful of the team's responsibility to make the ultimate decision.

The board chair's #1 rule for running the meetings is to remember that the teams are the experts within their area of expertise. While it's okay for the rest of the board to make suggestions or raise an issue on their presentations, the board chair should make sure that there are no protracted debates or long-winded discussions at board meetings. The teams will discuss any suggestions that originate from board member comments, but it's their choice whether to act on them or not.

As was recommended earlier, one of the board chair's primary goals should be to develop a culture of friendly competition between the various teams. As the competitive culture of the board grows, the teams will strive to match, or, at the very least, keep up with, the progress of the other teams. This competition is based on the premise that it's okay for board members to compete on a friendly basis. After all, a competitive culture plays an important role in the success of any entrepreneurial organization. It's up to the board chair, through the application of his team-building skills, to assure that the competition between teams remain friendly, productive and fun.

Now that you have your board assembled, the teams collaborating and the board chair and ED steering the ship, how can you measure your board's progress? Welcome to the world of KPIs.

Chapter 11
Recommended Goals for
Measuring the Effectiveness of the Board

"Having a CPA on your board will assure that your financial KPIs are the right ones."

Every successful organization, be it for-profit or nonprofit, has a mission. That mission, whether it is to eradicate poverty, educate kids or rescue animals is, in effect, the ultimate goal of the organization. However, there are many subsidiary goals that must be pursued in order for the organization to achieve its ultimate goal. These subsidiary goals are known as Key Performance Indicators in the for-profit world (aka KPIs). Some of the nonprofit's KPIs must be financial in nature (*no money, no mission*, remember?) and thus are easy to measure. Others are more organizational or cultural in nature, which means they are more subjective but every bit as important.

Financial KPIs can be the responsibility of the finance committee and could include such numbers as clients served, revenues generated, or expenses. Having a CPA on your board will assure that your financial KPI's are the right ones.

Following is a suggested list of subjective KPIs, followed by some guidelines on how to actually measure the KPI:

- Help the executive director succeed.

  This KPI should be measured in tandem by 1) the ED and 2) the board chair as he prepares the ED's performance review.

- Build a strong balance sheet.

  Is the nonprofit financially more sound than it was a year ago? This KPI should be measured by the finance team chair, using the same logistics that apply to a for-profit business.

- Develop a significant signature event.

  A *significant* signature event is defined as one which generates 8 (or you can pick a number) percent or more of the organization's annual budget. This KPI should be measured by the event team chair.

- Develop messaging that resonates within the community.

  Does the organization's messaging create the desired perception within the community? This KPI should be measured by a combination of the board chair, ED and marketing chair.

- Attract and properly recognize the organization's donors.

  Do the organization's fundraising efforts generate the amount of donations budgeted and are there effective stewardship programs in place to properly appreciate donors? This KPI should be measured by the fundraising chair.

- Develop increased community partnerships.

  Have the number and effectiveness of the collaborations with the organization's key community partners increased or decreased during the course of the prior year? This KPI should be measured by the board chair and the ED.

- Become the best board in the community.

  Obviously this KPI is impossible to measure, but it's certainly an inspirational goal to pursue. This KPI should be measured as best as possible (more on this below) by the board chair and the ED.

- Have fun.

  As discussed earlier, activities such as board meetings, events and projects are either fun or they aren't. If they aren't fun, good board members will leave. Thus, the fun factor can be partially measured by the organization's board member attrition rate. Lessons learned from exit interviews of departing board members can also provide an effective measurement tool. This KPI should be measured by the board chair and ED.

Criteria for Success

Reviewing the above list of KPIs, you'll note that none are purely financial. As a result, there must be significant subjectivity in their measurement. Most of the subjective measurements will be seen through the eyes of the beholder, i.e., the person doing the measuring. The beholder, however, should develop her own list of criteria to be used in measuring the subjective KPIs. For instance, in order to become the best board in the community, the board chair and the executive director could use any number of criteria that they believe to be important, such as:

- Input from the community's United Way executive director who, by virtue of his role in awarding monies to worthy nonprofit organizations, knows which of the community's nonprofits have effective boards and which do not.
- The number of board member attendees at the most recent fundraising event.
- The amount of money raised at the most recent fundraising event, in part, a function of board member involvement.
- The number of partnerships developed in the last reporting period.
- The strength of the balance sheet, accuracy in budgeting, and control of expenses.
- The number of volunteers in the previous reporting period.
- The number of clients served in the previous reporting period.
- Etc.

Measurement of the organization's KPIs should be a monthly, or at the very least quarterly, endeavor. The results of KPI measurement procedures should be included as part of the period-end financial statement package and should be disseminated to board members and staff members for use in determining ways to increase the organization's effectiveness.

What Will You Do?

Hopefully, if you've stayed with me this far, I've made the case for the entrepreneurial team concept and you're itching to begin transitioning your organization. The next step is to share this book with other key players on your prospective team, followed by publically announcing your organization's commitment to making the change. After that, there'll be no turning back.

Conclusion

The primary lesson I've learned in my 20 years serving on, and working with, nonprofit boards is that collectively they are the #1 underutilized asset in my community. I suspect that this is the case in your community as well. If true, it follows then that by upgrading the horsepower of our local nonprofit boards, we have the leverage to make more of a difference than with any other community-wide endeavor.

I've also learned over the course of a 30-year entrepreneurial career, which preceded my involvement with nonprofits, that the skills that entrepreneurs have, the educated risks they are willing to take, and their penchant for execution, are the key ingredients behind why the United States has the most vibrant for-profit economy in the world. The result of this conclusion is that I can't help but wonder what the result would be if we could combine the best traits of the entrepreneur with the nonprofit opportunity? What would ensue if we could mix and match the cool things that nonprofits do with the people whose role in life is to make things happen and get things done?

Making the connection between the entrepreneurial mindset and the nonprofit social mission is the sole purpose of this book. I challenge those entrepreneurs among you to make the same change in the nonprofit world that you've made in the for-profit one. I also challenge those of you who aren't entrepreneurs to find the right one to help you build your board. I know they're out there.

Think about it. What if all of us, using the concept of entrepreneurial teams as described in this book, could elevate the output of our nation's nonprofit organizations?

The opportunity boggles the mind, wouldn't you agree?

Note to the Reader

If you'd like to share your board-building experience with me as a result of reading this book, I'd love to hear from you. You can reach me at jim.schell5@gmail.com. Don't be shy. The Entrepreneurial Team Model is a work in progress, and, as we've learned from the likes of Wikipedia, the more cooks, the better the brew.

Hey there, and congratulations on reaching the end of this book—you are now prepared to better understand nonprofit boards and make your mark on the world. But before then, I would like to give you a chance to help me, and to help yourself in the process as well.

Reviews are the backbone of many successful books and, more importantly, a chance for you to have a direct impact on the content that I create in the future. I highly recommend that you take several moments to leave a review. I will personally read all of them and take them into careful consideration for future releases. You are helping to ensure that I create amazing content in the future that you will love.

Go to lightsonpublishing.com/feedback to leave a review—don't worry about length, spelling, grammar, or anything else for that matter, as the simple effort of leaving a review is what will allow me to continue to help you in the future.

Made in the USA
Columbia, SC
13 November 2017